The Toy Box

by Gabrielle Adams
illustrated by Eli Martin

Practice Pre-Decodable 4

Mc Graw Hill Education

Bothell, WA • Chicago, IL • Columbus, OH • New York, NY

MHEonline.com

Send all inquiries to:
McGraw-Hill Education
8787 Orion Place
Columbus, OH 43240

ISBN: 978-0-02-132203-9
MHID: 0-02-132203-1

Printed in the United States of America.

8 9 10 CTM 23

the 

car

a 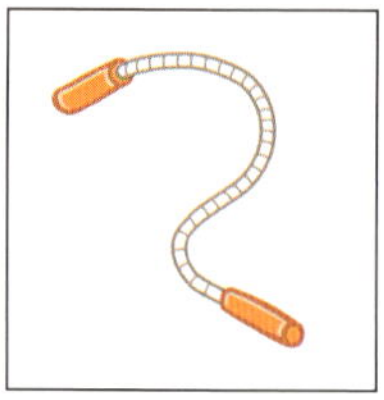

jump rope

the 

blocks

a 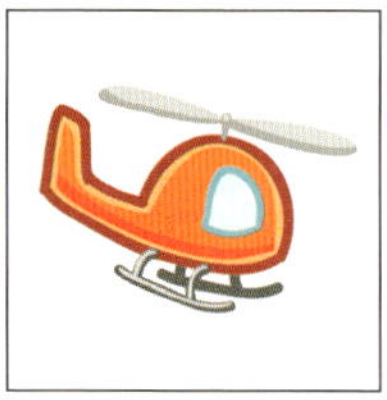

helicopter

the 

pig

the 

toy box